Table of Contents

Dedication

This reading is dedicated to God. I am forever thankful for all that I have experienced and all that is to come. To my C.H.A.N.G.E.D. Church family, especially Apostle Wallace and First Lady Laura. The clarity that all of you have brought me on my spiritual walk has allowed me to remain strong in my faith. Also, to my mother for her continued love and support.

Thank you!

Intro

I want to begin by stating that I am only writing this book to step in my kingdom's dispensation. I am not a fan of putting my business on blast. I am not looking for fame because I enjoy being able to walk around in public without scrutiny. I sat in a sermon recently and listened to the apostle speak about the hardships of life. I am a person that has known different kinds of troubles throughout my life. I have been poor, homeless, heartbroken, lonely, etc. Through it all, God was with me. By the grace of God, I am still alive and healthy, both physically and mentally. I knew that God had allowed me to be in times of struggle to protect me from the wrong path. I knew that these struggles would help get me on the right path. It wasn't until this particular sermon that I understood another reasoning for my struggles. My trials and tribulations were also placed upon me so that I may help others get through similar situations.

While I am a person that smiles through the pain. I pride myself on finding the good in any situation. I, on the other hand, am not one to be open about my personal life. To help others through my testimony, requires me to run my mouth. I hate running, unless I am running to the bank. Throughout my whole life, I knew two things were destined for me; that I would be a teacher and God had something great for me. So, as I listened to the sermon touch on the 5-fold ministry, I realized that desire to teach was not only for the educational system, but for the spiritual system as well. While I am Christian, I am not perfect; but always real.

Intimacy

Intimacy is more than just an exchange between two people. Intimacy by definition is close familiarity or closeness. It is being emotionally connected and supported. We often correlate intimacy with the level of sexual acts committed with another. In reality, one has a level of intimacy with every person and thing that they come in contact with. Most people lack a mutual intimacy with God. God is always on an intimate level with His people. He created each and every person. He knows each one, better than they know themselves. He knows the thoughts, the brokenness, and the needs of each and every person. It is us, however, that lack an intimate relationship with God. We walk around in doubt. We compete with others, in fear that someone will have one up on us. Not knowing that God knows our needs and will provide what we need. We get caught in chasing what society has sold as the definition of success and feel incomplete in the process of obtaining it. In reality, our emptiness is caused because we are chasing something that is not truly for us. It will not fulfill our spirit because it is not the fuel needed to keep us running.

We often look at hardships as God leaving and/or deceiving us. When in actuality it is His way of showing that He has chosen us. Being chosen is the beginning of God's favor. When you are chosen, what is blessed is blessed; and what is cursed is cursed. Society will tell you that your actions are a direct representation of your value, and your treatment will correlate directly with your value. For example, if you are caught in a scandal, then you become less valued, and therefore, deserve lesser treatment. God does not operate on the same basis. God does not let what you've been through change your value. He understands that royalty is still royalty; strength is still strength. He understands that when he chooses you that blessings will overpower any trial you've been through. He understands the power of His curse brought upon anyone who wrongs His people. For that alone, God deserves our intimacy. Intimacy is built allowing God to rule your court, house, and temple.

Allowing God to rule your court is to allow God to have justice. I recall always wanting vengeance for something that someone had done to either me or my loved ones. It wasn't until I let go and let God, did I start to see mountains being moved for me. I was in my late 20s-early 30s when I had learned this lesson. I stopped worrying about having the one up in relationships, getting my get back, and still truths were revealed to me. I was engaged in a relationship and still scarred from a previous marriage. I told myself that in my new relationship, I would not go through phones. I would use better communication skills when disagreeing. Still, I was given the short end of the stick. I was dealing with a dishonest man and his bitter mother. I was walking with God. It was revealed to me the dangers that this man was tied to. God had better for me.

Throughout my life I had received plenty of speeding tickets. It has always been in me to speed. It sits right in my spirit. Each time a ticket was given, it put me in a financial burden. I felt that I was being punished. I asked why would God give me the need for speed, just to give me fines when I do what was put in me? I learned to speed with caution. I learned to speed and blend in as needed to avoid any further citations. While dealing with the dishonest man that I previously mentioned, a dangerous situation occurred while my children were present. While fleeing that situation, I was chased by an opposing car. Had it not been for the speeding and the tickets, I would have never been able to get away from that car chase.

> "The Lord has gifted Bezalel, Oholiab, and the other skilled craftsmen with wisdom and ability to perform any task involved in building the sanctuary. Let them construct and furnish the Tabernacle, just as the Lord has commanded."

> -Exodus 36:1

God will put in your heart the skills needed. In that situation, I was wronged by every party involved, but I understood that the justice belonged to God. The old me would have been focused on starting a war, especially being that my kids were involved, however, I let God rule my court. I watched God fight that battle in which I watched each person involved beg for mercy.

Being that no one is bigger than the Almighty, a war amongst His people is one that no one is prepared for.

Another level of intimacy comes when one allows God to rule the house. The house is a place where one discovers the satisfaction and demands of exchanges. Allowing God to clean house is always the hardest for me. Often, we are taught that with faith we can call on God and he will answer our prayers. What we are not taught is that to have our prayers answered, an exchange is often made. We are often required to give up a piece of ourselves to have those prayers answered. We often put worldly things before our spirituality. It's common for people to idolize money, fame, love, envy, etc.

"You must not bow down to them or worship them, for I, the Lord your God, am a jealous God who will not tolerate your affection for any other gods. I lay the sins of the parents upon their children; the entire family is affected—even children in the third and fourth generations of those who reject me."

It is stated that God is a jealous God. He also will let His wrath be felt amongst generations of those that idolize others. Is it realistic to think that this same God will answer the prayers of someone who values fame more than their relationship with Him? God is vain and appreciates seeing Himself in those that He created. I had offended God when I chose to cherish my marriage more than my relationship Him. I had made my marriage an idol. I did all that I could to prevent my marriage from failing. Yet, the harder I worked on that marriage, the more struggles we had. In my previous marriage, my then husband was not a man lead by faith, so when then rain came, we floated different ways. By definition intimacy is defined as a closeness, familiarity, and friendship built with another individual. So, I spent time building intimacy with an individual before building intimacy with God. Had I built that intimacy with God, I would have been able to identify the traits of God with ease. I would have known God as more than the ruler and the authority father figure, but also known Him as friend. I would have known Him as the comfort on a lonely night. I would have known Him as more than the provider, but also as the leader. I would have known Him as the healer, not just physically, but emotionally. Building that intimacy with God was needed before I stepped out in the dating world because I would have been able to recognize with God's traits within potential mates. At the time of my marriage, I knew God to lead with authority and a provider, causing me to choose a man that was providing and an authoritarian. As years passed, there was a deeper intimacy that I needed as the storms grew bigger. I had the belief that love was enough to fight any battle. God continued to destroy any home that was built on the foundation of love because that was not the foundation I needed. It wasn't until I built on the foundation of intimacy with the Lord that I began to see change.

"They were snatched away in the prime of life, the foundations of their lives washed away."

-Job 22:16

After my divorce, I began to yearn for God. My relationship with Him grew stronger. He is my foundation. He is my template for life. In result to that intimacy, I changed my social circle accordingly. Learning God to be a friend, allowed the ability to choose better friends. Learning God as healer, allowed me to surround myself with people that will pray during spiritual turmoil. Knowing God as the protector, helped me choose people that will not go to war with me, but for me.

"With praise and thanks, they sang this song to the Lord: 'He is so good! His faithful love for Israel endures forever!' Then all the people gave a great shout, praising the Lord because the foundation of the Lord's Temple had been laid."

-Ezra 3:11

Lack of Lack

I went through life often feeling as if I was given the short end of the stick. My family was dysfunctional. I watched a failed married, with a father with children from multiple women, and siblings with autism. Financially, my family struggled more than my peers. I had experienced sexual assault and had a temper that was uncontrollable. For what it is worth, I do not have a financially beneficial talent. Statistically, I was destined for failure. I was dysfunctional the definition of lack, yet somehow, I ended up with blessings.

The reason for this is that with God there isn't a such thing as lack. Everything that one goes through truly builds one for the life journey that they will go through. Part of the struggles that one will have is determined by the type of anointing has on their life. I watched my parents' marriage fail at the age of ten. I was old enough to understand the what infidelity was, but also close enough to both parents to understand the nature of the actions amongst both parties. This prepared me for the life I would have. In my own marriage, I watched history repeat the same cycle. While I married with love in my heart, our vows failed because God was not at the center of our marriage. During that marriage, I felt lack. I felt I was lacking financially, emotionally, and spiritually. The truth is at that time the only thing that I was lacking was the faith in God to turn it around in my favor.

"'For the Lord your God has blessed you in everything you have done. He has watched your every step through this great wilderness. During these forty years, the Lord your God has been with you, and you have lacked nothing.'"

-Deuteronomy 2:7

Throughout my life, I watched God turn nothing into everything that was needed. When we went through a stage of homelessness, God used the same family dynamic to bless us with a home. I moved to Los Angeles, just to lose a job. God blessed me with a new job that paid enough for me to live alone. When the year Covid came around, I was an hourly employee, post-divorce, living back at home with my mom and children. While many were losing jobs and homes, God blessed me with my home owning opportunity and a new career.

There was never a time that I was lacking anything. I had to learn to maneuver in faith. Faith is built on trust. It is difficult to trust God when you have learned to distrust people. People lie. People manipulate. People lack power and knowledge. God is not a person. He is the almighty. Where people lie, God is the truth. Whereas people lack power, God is power. God is the all-knowing.

"The Lord is my strength and my song; he has given me victory. This is my God, and I will praise him— my father's God, and I will exalt him!"

-Exodus 15:2

It is only when you walk in faith with God that you will understand His ability to conquer all. While walking in faith with God will cause you to understand that there is a lack of lack. Everything that you need God will provide, in His timing. His timing in the perfect timing. When you walk with God, instead of ahead of God, peace enters your life. Worry disappears. That is not a guarantee that life will be perfect.

> "You have armed me with strength for
> the battle; you have subdued my enemies
> under my feet."

-Psalm 18:39

The Attack

So, there I was. Aligned and focused on God. Was I completely obedient? No. If I had followed what God had spoken over my life, then I would have never flown back to California. It is not that I did not trust God's plan. It was that I did not trust my ability to hear God clearly. I did not trust my ability to discern. I flew back to California with a new since of purpose. My mind set on ministry, my heart on God, I expected the next year to be a breeze. I was wrong! I will never know if I had stayed in Florida would my life been less chaotic, but I do know my school year in California was met unbearable conditions.

I walked onto my school campus in good spirits. I had organized my school lessons ahead of time so that my schedule would allow for me to write, minister, and grow in God. I started my day with prayer and joined the rest of my coworkers for our developmental training. It was in our training that I was informed that a student would be inappropriately placed in my class. The student was over 250 pounds, taller than 5'8, and used aggressive behaviors as a way to communicate. The student's cognitive abilities were significantly lower than any of the other students in my class. This was alarming to me because the first day of school was the following day and I did not have enough time to prepare for the student. I was not too alarmed by the change, just annoyed at the lack of consideration on the behalf of the district. I knew I was protected by the blood, so I knew that all would work in my favor.

> "There the child grew up healthy and strong.
> He was filled with wisdom, and
> God's favor was on him."

> -Luke 2:40

The first day of school, I was informed by the student's former teacher that the discussion of placing the student in my class was discussed the previous school year. Had I been informed of this decision; I would not have returned to that school to be a teacher. The district waited until my contract went into effect to inform me of their decision. I felt disrespected. I prayed frequently. The more I prayed, the worse the situation got.

I felt that I was under a spiritual attack. I was stressed. Eventually, I was injured on the job. My district had not protected me, my union was not protecting me, and at the time I felt like God was not protecting me.

"Do not rebel against the Lord, and don't be afraid of the people of the land. They are only helpless prey to us! They have no protection, but the Lord is with us! Don't be afraid of them!"

-Numbers 14:9

I cried daily. I cried until I stopped fighting. I had to sit with God and remember my goal was to be obedient. I had to be honest with myself, and admit that me working for that school district was disobedience. I knew that (also, confirmed by prophecy) I was to minister through books and would become a business owner. I was doing neither. When that realization came to the forefront, I chose to give everything to God. I knew I had to step out on faith. I did not know how I would pay my mortgage on my empty home. I did not know how I would pay the rent in the current apartment. I did not care. I knew God would provide. I wrote my letter of resignation and planned for an exit at the end of the semester. With that one step of faith, things turned around.

"He has sent me to tell those who mourn that the time of the Lord's favor has come, and with it, the day of God's anger against their enemies."

-Isaiah 61:2

The following day, I was called into a meeting in the district office. I walked into the meeting physically and emotionally in pain, yet prepared to officially turn in my resignation. I was met instead with a blessing and God's protection. The district had made the decision to put me on paid leave for my injuries. GLORY BE TO GOD!!!! This paid leave allowed me to get everything in order. It allowed me an opportunity to heal fully. It allowed me to workout every morning. I had the opportunity to take my kids to school in the morning and be a full-time hands-on parent. I was blessed with the opportunity to establish the life that God placed upon me. I had freedom to write. I had freedom to look into opportunities to start the business. I had the freedom to serve at church more. I was blessed. It was at that time that I realized that what I thought was a demonic attack was not an attack at all. I thought God had put me in a season of Job, but in reality, he never allowed the enemy to attack me. He had to have me surrender in obedience to receive what He had for me.

Sometimes, we will curse the devil in thoughts of being under attack. We will be in the battle of our life and doubt our authority when in reality, we give the devil too much credit. We will fall to out knees, sacrifice, and still struggle. Only God has that kind on power over our lives. My rule now is if I have prayed and praised over a situation then I humble myself to ask God what is it that I need to do to appease Him. The change needed can range from service, change of action, to sit still and listen, or take accountability and repent.

> "And now, Israel, what does the Lord your God require of you? He requires only that you fear the Lord your God, and live in a way that pleases him, and love him and serve him with all your heart and soul."
>
> -Deuteronomy 10:12

The easiest change God can ask for is to serve Him. The ease comes from God asking for your service in the areas that he has gifted you in. The hardest part of service is putting one's pride to the side and identifying what God has blessed you in versus what you want to be blessed in. I want to be a great event planner. I want to be organized and social enough to host weddings, food drives, and networking events. Over the years, I was passionate about dance, but I was not the greatest at it. I spent years trying to find my gift. There are a few things I knew about myself that came easy. I can work with special needs children well and I others find me easy to talk to. What could I possibly do with that? How could I possibly give the glory to God with that?

It took months of prayers for it to be revealed that my gifts are not to be used together, but separate and for different reasons. One gift was to be used to give back to the community, while the other was to serve the church directly.

"But be sure to fear the Lord and
faithfully serve him. Think of
all the wonderful things he has done for you."

-1 Samuel 12:24

I tend to be a warm and welcoming individual. Not because I am a great person, but because God placed understanding in me. He let me witness all walks of life to understand that not all high earners are saved, and those in humble beginnings are not less than. I myself have been a humbled by God and will forever be grateful to that season. It is these characteristics that qualified me to be a greeter in my church (Lord knows singing is not my gift). I started serving with gratitude and my line of service blessed me even more. While serving, God gave me a chance to build on my prophetic ability. I would listen to God and see if I decorated the greeting table's colors to align with the colors of the Apostle and First Lady or the worship flags used that day. As I grew in my faith, my prophetic ability became greater. As I grew in my faith, I began to feel the anointing placed upon me.

"Those who fight against the Lord will be shattered. He thunders against them from heaven; the Lord judges throughout the earth. He gives power to his king; he increases the strength of his anointed one."

-1 Samuel 2:10

The Anointing

My struggles lessened when I learned the anointing that I had placed on my life. In reality, the struggles placed upon are life are allowed to happen for character development amongst ourselves. In order to be truly thankful for the struggle, that will later bring a blessing, one must enter a stage of reframing.

Spiritual reframing is a technique used to shift the way that Christians interpret negativity and affliction. The process of spiritual reframing is to become faith centered and stand in that faith during tough times. In that stance, you must avoid agreement with any negativity. As a Christian, you hold power in your tongue and that power of the tongue has a capacity. So, if you are in agreement with debt, you are no longer leaving space for financial blessings. While attending C.H.A.N.G.E.D Church, I was educated about the four negative thoughts that can prevent your spiritual reframing.

The first negative thought is grounding. Grounding is the belief that miracles and wonders cannot happen for you. This thought should not hold true in any believers' heart.

> "Now all glory to God, who is able, through his mighty power at work within us, to accomplish infinitely more than we might ask or think."
>
> -Ephesians 3:20

God is able to do exceedingly abundant things. He can do it all, but he will not allow it to happen until you are ready to receive and give Him the glory. The second negative thought is that you are condemned and do not deserve what God has to offer. It is easy to understand this negative thought. God is the amazing almighty. Nothing that we do for Him can ever be enough to thank Him for all that He has done. I often fell into this negative thought when I had backslid into a behavior that I promised God that I would remove from my life. How could I go and have a night out and then face God and ask Him for anything? Even after repentance, how could He want to bless me after direct disobedience?

> "And God will generously provide all you need. Then you will always have everything you need and plenty left over to share with others."

> -2 Corinthians 9:8

God is able to place grace upon you. That same repentance that brought guilt upon me, is what allows God to bring forgiveness and grace. The third negative thought is limitations. Grounding is the belief that God is not able, whereas limitations is the belief that you, yourself are not capable of carrying what God has placed upon you. This is closely related to negative thought number four, the feeling of disqualified. Disqualification happens when one feels they do not have enough knowledge or talent to accomplish success in the ministry that God has called them to.

"But when the Father sends the Advocate as my representative—that is, the Holy Spirit—he will teach you everything and will remind you of everything I have told you."

-John 14:26

God will send the Holy Spirit, to teach you all things. These negative thoughts are easier to push past when one understands their anointing.

There are many different anointings that are mentioned in the bible. When figuring out which anointing represents oneself, take in consideration how and why that anointing was placed upon them. While going through my struggles, I felt I was embodying Job. Everything that could go wrong, was going extremely wrong. The difference between my afflictions and those of Job is Job's afflictions came from the faith that he had in God, whereas mine came from disobedience. Even though there are many different anointings, I am going to discuss the two that flow through me. I am a combination of the Abrahamic and Davidic anointings.

The Abrahamic anointing is one that requires a string sense of faith. As every blessing that Abraham received required an act of faith. The signs that you are blessed with the Abrahamic anointing are:

- Your life looks contrary to the word of your life.
- Missed blessings
- Generations of unfilled dreams
- Humbleness

I found all of these situations to be true to my life. My life was not what I knew it should be. I knew that I am a woman of God and I shall not struggle for ever. I knew that I was destined for greatness. I knew poverty, sadness, anger, and defeat were not the calling for my life because God could not get the glory from those situations. Most importantly, some of my biggest blessings came from moving in faith. I moved to another city, without a source of income or a place to stay, with the basis that God would provide. I was employed with my own one-bedroom apartment by the grace of God. I applied to my master's program at California Baptist University without the required G.P.A and was admitted to the program of choice and graduated with success. That same program required me to student teach or find an internship before graduation. Student teaching required me to work underneath another teacher as a teacher without the pay. Interning, allowed me to teach my own classroom, with pay, and have check-ins with a mentor teacher. I was a mother and primary provider for two children. The hindrance that I had was that my undergraduate degree was not in education. The chances of me landing an internship were slim. I applied as many internship positions as possible, including ones at the school I was working as an aide. When I was denied by the school that I was employed by, I felt discouraged, but I kept the faith that God would work it out. Two weeks before I was set to student-teach I was offered an internship by a neighboring district. Praises to God. Even though I had been denied a home loan multiple times, I stepped out on faith and applied for a home loan. I was unsure if my credit was good enough; I was unsure if my income was acceptable. I did not even have a down payment, but I stood in faith and was able to buy a home. This anointing requires you to empty yourself and allow God in. To receive your blessings, pray that God fills your vessel with Him. That the Holy Spirit enters you and embodies Jesus Christ. That your embodiment becomes a walking testimony that allows God to get the glory. It is that same emptiness that gives you purpose. It is important that those with the Abrahamic anointing remain humble in their success.

"even though I have received such wonderful revelations from God. So, to keep me from becoming proud, I was given a thorn in my flesh, a messenger from Satan to torment me and keep me from becoming proud.

8 Three different times I begged the Lord to take it away. 9 Each time he said, "My grace is all you need. My power works best in weakness." So now I am glad to boast about my weaknesses, so that the power of Christ can work through me. 10 That's why I take pleasure in my weaknesses, and in the insults, hardships, persecutions, and troubles that I suffer for Christ. For when I am weak, then I am strong."

-2 Corinthians 12:7-10

God will allow you to have a weakness and it is that weakness that allows Christ's power within you.

The Davidic anointing is different than that of Abraham. The Davidic anointing is rooted in battle, affliction, and courage. Signs of the Davidic anointing are having at least four of the eight:

- Strained paternal relationship
- Loneliness
- Intelligence or courage that is undermined
- Gifts in poetry, music, or song
- Temper and/or high libido
- Masters at repenting
- Inclination of the prophetic or prophetic dreams
- Cycles of almost giving up

The Davidic anointing wrong true to my heart because I have repeatedly experienced six of the eight qualifiers of the anointing. I experience patterns of strained relationships with both of my parents. It is a difficult place to be in to relate more to my father and be physically distanced from him, while relying on an emotionally distanced mother to pick up the pieces. The loneliness does not end with paternal figures, yet extends to family and friends as well.

My siblings either have autism or life views that are self-centered. Autism makes it hard for individuals to bond as close as neuro-typical individuals often do. Being my mother's oldest child, I focused of family goals, so I find it difficult to understand the need to focus on self-goals or not helping others. I knew from a young age that my brothers would eventually become my responsibility. That burden made it difficult for me to relate to my peers. When I did form friendships, it was often at a surface level because my struggles were not ones that other children could relate to. Many of my friends were living for the now, where as I was living for the future.

The only time that I lived in the moment was during my high school years. Previous to my high school years, I focused on being a well-rounded individual. I wanted to know as much as I could to make sure that I could provide for my siblings in the event that my parents passed. I was in gifted/honors classes with excelling grades. In high school, I dropped out of honors classes with the focus of experiencing life as much as I could. I often didn't participate in class, complete homework, nor attend class as much as I should have. Being placed in general education classes, I passed classes because I had previously learned the material in the honors program. My giftedness was often overlooked. Many saw me as a typical black girl, but I was respectful, so teachers passed me and never took time to see the talent I had. My dance teacher and my 9th grade English teacher were the only teachers I had that invested time into me. They were the only ones that knew I could play an instrument, make a song out of anything, and was great at remember facts.

There was a flip side to my greatness. I am a fighter to the core. My patience was low and my temper was bad. I was not one to disrespect because I was quick to catch someone after school. I did not care how big someone was, nor their sex; I would come swinging if I felt I was wronged. My mouth was slick and I was always ready for war.

As I became an adult, I learned that there was a time in place for everything. I could not just throw hands with my manager because I did not like the manner in which they spoke to me. My battles became less physical, and more mental. Every day became a chess battle. I was fighting financially, spiritually, emotionally. I missed the physicality of fighting. I missed the heart racing fury. I missed the physical competition. I soon learned to replace that feeling with sexual fulfillment. I was dating for lust, not for a purpose or love. My need for conquer could compete with the most masculine of men. I only dated those who I knew could compete with me. It soon became a cycle. Rough day led to spending time with my partner, leading to sexual activity, leading to small accomplishment, leading to a lack of feeling fulfilled in life. Learning about my Davidic anointment helped me break this cycle become aware of life and living. The Davidic anointing is a lifestyle of victory through adversity.

"Have you seen the giant?" the men asked. "He comes out each day to defy Israel. The king has offered a huge reward to anyone who kills him. He will give that man one of his daughters for a wife, and the man's entire family will be exempted from paying taxes!" 26 David asked the soldiers standing nearby, "What will a man get for killing this Philistine and ending his defiance of Israel? Who is this pagan Philistine anyway, that he is allowed to defy the armies of the living God?" 27 And these men gave David the same reply. They said, "Yes, that is the reward for killing him."

-1 Samuel 17:25-27

The Davidic anointing is rooted in courage. God does not send you into to battle to lose but to show how great He is when you stand with Him. If the odds aren't against you then it was not sent by

God. I also had to learn to be true to myself. I was built for every battle given to me. All of my life I was known for leading, dominating, fighting, and high levels of energy. It was those same God given qualities that will help me in times of need. This anointing will cause a life of victory over giant battles/struggles, overcoming demonic traps, and a need to restore after spiritual mistakes. In all of these battles, you must remain focused on the Lord and resist from letting the world harden you. Understand that there will be victory and that victory. In times of struggle when I feel the need to give up, I pray,

"God, I come before you asking you for forgiveness for any and everything that I have done that has disappointed you. Lord, I am at a crossroads that I know you will use to glorify your name. I am here asking, what is it that you want me to do? Please reveal to me if I am in the way of my next miracle. As I stand with you, remove those who do not believe in your power. Make me uncomfortable in mediocrity, as I know that is not what you have for me. Lord reveal to me what is needed and allow me to act in obedience. In Jesus name, amen."

Everything you experience under this anointing is necessary to bring you closer to God. When I felt like running from an individual who tried to make a false claim to Child Protective Services (C.P.S), I was welcomed at a church that later became my church home. When I was fighting against an unfair work environment, I found peace in serving the Lord in that church. When I started to lose friends, I gained a supportive church family. All of those situations were set to be demonic traps.

"But you have received the Holy Spirit, and he lives within you, so you don't need anyone to teach you what is true. For the Spirit teaches you everything you need to know, and what he teaches is true—it is not a lie. So just as he has taught you, remain in fellowship with Christ.",
-1 John 2:27

The anointing is there, so that prevents deception. The hardest struggle of the Davidic anointing is knowing that God will bring you through it.

"The Lord gives both death and life; he brings some down to the grave but raises others up.7 The Lord makes some poor and others rich; he brings some down and lifts others up."
-1 Samuel 2:6-7

During hard times it is important to remember God has the power. He can bring you through anything. He is the ultimate good. Every trial that you experience will help develop your character for the blessings that he will bring into your life. How God uses you is unique to the experiences that you will have in your life. God gives us our kingdom dispensation, or assignment for our lives and our ministry. A kingdom dispensation is often the intertwining of our anointing and our skill/talent. It is often difficult to determine what a true skill is because in a capitalist society, we are often focused of skills that are easy routes to making money. This is problematic because capitalist views do not align with the power of God. If God seeks to have fortune and wealth in your life, it will happen no matter what your skill is. People that sit in art exhibits reading, with millions of viewers are an example of God's greatness. A more common example is the YouTubers that make millions from streaming their videogames. Our skills/talents are often ordained in your childhood atmosphere.

It took me years to understand my assignment. By capitalist viewpoint, I am a black woman that came from divorced parents, with multiple siblings with developmental delays. I grew up in a town that was predominately occupied with white two parent homes. So, by America's viewpoint, my best option was to go to college to make a living from my experience with understanding atypical backgrounds and family dynamics. Common job descriptions for my capitalist talent would be counselor, teacher, psychologist, etc. However, using my experiences in a spiritual manner opened the doors for much more. My divorced parents left me to grow up without the funds to have proper resources to complete homework. So, while my peers were using a computer to complete their assignments, I was using a typewriter. While my peers were able to use the backspace button to correct their mistakes, I had to rewrite a whole page of my essay any time I made a mistake. God was using that for character development. I became a master at identifying and correcting writing. What capitalistic society would identify as a teaching qualification, spiritually I was qualified as a clerk, teacher, editor, and author. God multiplied my qualifications with that experience. I had multiple siblings with developmental delays. My understanding of the mind's functional abilities is greater than those without this experience. I am able to teach things to many individuals. My communication abilities are a strength because I am able to understand receptive language and express ideas at many levels. Causing me to notice slight energy changes in atmospheres. By society's standards, I have the natural qualifications of a teacher or behavioral therapist. Yet, by spiritual qualifications, I can also utilize my talents for advocacy, designer, speech therapist, and business owner. My experience understanding different racial viewpoints allows for me to move amongst the masses.

My kingdom dispensation allows me to minister to the unheard. It allows me to Teach others that even though it may seem as if you are overlooked or forgotten by God, your story is not over. Every situation that you will encounter was necessary for the growth and development for your story. No matter your anointing you will have rescues.

"The Lord gives his people strength. He is a safe fortress for his anointed king."
-Psalm 28:8

The Cry and Silence

We as Christians go through a cycle. We pray. We cry. We see victory. We are often taught that because we are believers, that our prayers will be answered. The mistake that we make is that our prayers will be answered immediately. We pray without listening for an answer. It is our human nature to talk twice as much as we listen, not realizing that we are looking for answer that is from the spiritual realm. It is then that we are often met with the silence of God.

To humans, silence is synonymous with one not listening and/or one not being interested in what was said. We as humans have a strong distain for silence because it is a direct strike to our ego. Spiritually, the silence of God is a sign of wisdom and self-control. It is unnecessary for God to continuously go back in forth with his children when He is the all-knowing. God uses His silence to build character within us. He uses his silence in three occurrences:

- To make one rely on his last response
- To test faith
- As mercy and grace

Though the silence of God can make one feel forsaken, we must remember the message from the last encounter we had with God.

An encounter with God is an event where one feels a deep connection or interaction with God. This could be from the results of prayer, dreams, or a strong discernment of a message put on your heart. While opposing forces have access to your prayers and can relay messages to you, it is important to mature your relationship with God to decipher the difference. I learned to through Apostle Wallace, the apostle of C.H.A.N.G.E.D Church, that encounters with God will have one of four outcomes:

- Exceptional endorsement of God
- Inner transformation
- Release to a new dimension
- Divine intervention/miracle

With each encounter with God, it is progressive. We start with the exceptional endorsement of God.

"Then a voice from the cloud said, 'This is my Son, my Chosen One. Listen to him'."

-Luke 9:35

When we accept Jesus as our Lord and Savior, we sent with him on the throne. His authority flows through us. So just as God said in the book of Luke, we will have that same authority. If we do not accept Jesus, then we will not receive the mercy and grace of God. Those who do not follow God will not enter the gates of heaven.

"Not everyone who calls out to me, 'Lord! Lord!' will enter the Kingdom of Heaven. Only those who actually do the will of my Father in heaven will enter. 22 On judgment day many will say to me, 'Lord! Lord! We prophesied in your name and cast out demons in your name and performed many miracles in your name.' 23 But I will reply, 'I never knew you. Get away from me, you who break God's laws.'

-Matthew 7:21-23

The next progressive step in an encounter from God is the inner transformation.

"'What is your name?" the man asked. He replied, "Jacob." **28** "Your name will no longer be Jacob," the man told him. "From now on you will be called Israel, because you have fought with God and with men and have won."

-Genesis 32:27-28

An encounter with God can leave us with a new outlook or mindset on life. When I was in the midst of losing my income, losing my house, and being publicly embarrassed in front of my peers, I went to church and began to speak in heavenly tongue. That encounter with God removed the worry that I had for my loss, knowing that God would replace not only what I loss, but also increase in every area of loss that I suffered. God wants the trust knowing that He can provide all of our needs. Yet, just as exceptional endorsement, there is a negative outcome for not accepting the inner transformation that God offers. Many of us reject the transformation out of disobedience and battle with God. It is a battle we will always lose, but our ego makes us think we are able to persuade God to change His word just for us. It is the battle that leads to the cry.

The cry is a public declaration to God that you are leading in faith, yet still in need for God to hear you. The tears themselves are presented in the physical realm as water that articulates what the soul expresses in the spiritual realm. It is the tears in the cry that seeds your spiritual expected ending. We often cry out to God wanting him to listen to our pleas, yet, his silence does not equate to His lack of hearing. Hearing is the process of taking in audio waves and their sensation of a sound stimulus. Listening is the perception that occurs after hearing. His silence to our cry is often a requirement for an increase in faith for God to move on our behalf.

"**17** The Lord hears his people when they call to him for help. He rescues them from all their troubles. **18** The Lord is close to the brokenhearted; he rescues those whose spirits are crushed. **19** The righteous person faces many troubles, but the Lord comes to the rescue each time."

–Psalm 34:17-19

The level of one's faith is directedly linked to their level of righteousness. It is that faith and righteousness that makes your tears matter to God. It is the righteousness that encourages Him to move on your behalf.

"But people are counted as righteous, not because of their work, but because of their faith in God who forgives sinners."

– Romans 4:5

It is also that faith that causes you to expect things to manifest for the better. Your results should be expected because of the tears you cried. When the soul is overwhelmed physically, tears are formed. Spiritually, those tears plant seeds that will harvest blessings. Those same tears, God will use to manifest the greatest areas of one's blessings.

> "'For I know the plans I have for you,' says the Lord. 'They are plans for good and not for disaster, to give you a future and a hope."
>
> – Jeremiah 29:11

God will recognize four categories of tears. He will recognize tears from:

- Desperation of faith
- Spiritual travail
- An undiscerned breakthrough
- Gratefulness

> "You keep track of all my sorrows. You have collected all my tears in your

bottle. You have recorded each one in your book."

– Psalm 56:8

God will keep track of every tear you to manifest your blessings. While it may be hard to keep the faith, it is necessary to remain chosen in the heavens. During a spiritual turmoil in my life, I prayed,

"God while I know you are still good; I ask that you record my misery. List my tears on your scroll because I know that you will use these tears to turn this situation around for your glory. My faith is so strong in you Father, that I ask for more travail God because that same travail will make me desperate for you. Through seeking you, I will always find the answer. If my words do no justice, hear my heart. Through the blood of Jesus, amen."

The prayer will not only gain the attention of God and have Him move on your behalf, but will also release you into a new dimension.

Being released into a new dimension is another progressive outcome in your encounter with God. My first notable release into a new dimension occurred when after I changed my outlook on church and fellowship. I have always been a believer. The life experiences I had and the feelings I had while praying confirmed that God is real. I always believed that my journey with was just that, MY JOURNEY. I believed that if my journey was personal, then I was covered to fellowship alone. This was a belief that I stood strong on. In the midst of losing my home, I felt that my prayers were enough. The spiritual travail worsened; I started to deal with an unfair workload in my career. I cried, I prayed, I anointed my home. The spiritual travail worsened. I came to realize that I was dating a narcissistic individual. One that a therapist told me that he feared for my safety. I shouted, cried, prayed, and was willing to sacrifice a goat all for things to get better. The thing that God spoke to me was to go to the church. I was so stuck on my ideology, that it led me to disobedience. The tears flowed every night. They flowed until my only option was to follow through on an invite to church.

I was physically ill from the nervousness that I felt. I am a person true to my David anointing. I am content in being alone and strongly despise new social situations. Before I had the chance to turn around, I seen my realtor turned friend at the doors. I entered reluctantly and sat towards the back. I did not plan on introducing myself, nor going to the alter for ANY reason. Halfway through the service the Holy Ghost overtook me. I had tears flowing down my face while having my first experience speaking in my heavenly language. It was my release into a new dimension.

"For our dying bodies must
be transformed into bodies that will never
die; our mortal bodies must
be transformed into immortal bodies."

– 1 Corinthians 15:53

At that moment the victories of those I was fellowshipping with became available for my access. The praises that were in the atmosphere brought the presence of God in a way that I could not do alone. My tears were heard because I had entered a new dimension. Speaking in tongue sent my communication straight to God.

> "For if you have the ability to speak in tongues, you will be talking only to God, since people won't be able to understand you. You will be speaking by the power of the Spirit, but it will all be mysterious."
>
> - 1 Corinthians 14:2

That new level of spirituality kept me focused on my spiritual journey. The more focused I became, the more my blessings arose. The toxic person disappeared without following on any of his threats. An opportunity presented itself to pay for my house while, I lived in a second location without financially struggling. My toxic job eventually paid for me to stay home. With all of those blessings God received the glory and the praise. Leading to my first prophetic vision.

After approximately a year from speaking in my heavenly language, I was serving in church and a woman with a black purse caught my attention. Her purse appeared to have a haze around it. I know that in the physical realm, the haze was not present, but at that moment I was tapped in to the spiritual realm. I continuously looked at the purse and felt the spirit of financial increase. The combination of my introverted personality and lack of prophecy expertise made me uneasy with revealing what God was telling me. I knew God directing to tell the woman that she was due for a financial increase, and I had enough wisdom to just obey God. Within a few minutes of speaking with the woman Apostle Wallace, a man that flows in the prophetic announced to that same woman that she would be receiving a financial increase on her job. That confirmation from a prophet was validation that I had entered yet a new dimension.

The last progressive step in an encounter with God is a divine intervention or miracle. Divine intervention and miracles come when God is able to use an individual. God will only use you when your heart posture is aligned with His agenda. To align with God's prerequisites of victory you must posses the seven spirits od God. This leads to the death of the worldly personality that one has acquired, and the intake of the true movement of God.

"Then, when our dying bodies have been transformed into bodies that will never die, this Scripture will be fulfilled: "Death is swallowed up in victory"

-1 Corinthians 15:54

Milk and Honey

In the cycle of Christianity, praying is followed by crying, which is followed by victory. When we have acquired all seven spirits of God, it is then that He will use an individual and allow them to enter you into the victorious season of milk and honey. The seven spirits of God are:

- Wisdom
- Understanding
- Counsel
- Might
- Fear of the Lord
- Knowledge
- Faith/Obedience

"2 And the spirit of the Lord shall rest upon him, the spirit of wisdom and understanding, the spirit of counsel and might, the spirit of knowledge and of the fear of the Lord;3 And shall make him of quick understanding in the fear of the Lord: and he shall not judge after the sight of his eyes, neither reprove after the hearing of his ears:4 But with righteousness shall he judge the poor, and reprove with equity for the meek of the earth: and he shall smite the earth: with the rod of his mouth, and with the breath of his lips shall he slay the wicked."

-Isaiah 11: 2-4

Many of the seven spirits coincide with another of the seven spirits. It is the fear of the Lord that will give you the might to fight the battles that come your way. If you know the power of God, then you know that nothing is more powerful, therefore, if God is for you who can be against you. It is that same knowledge of God that allows you to understand His movement amongst His people. In continuance, it is the counsel that He brings forth that allows you wisdom from the afflictions of others, that only His grace saved you from. The last being faith and obedience. It is only with faith can stand in obedience while your world is in turmoil and temptations increase.

Personally, God started to use me after I lost battles that I was having with God. I was born a hard-head and strong willed. I wanted to do what I wanted, when I wanted. I would argue with God on where I lived, who I dated, and getting vengeance on those who wronged me. It wasn't until God showed me that He was God, the Almighty, that I learned that the might that I was using to go against God was actually placed in me to fight the giants like David. As I gained knowledge about the miracles of God, is when I stopped questioning His movements in my life and learned to praise Him ahead of the blessings. It was at that time that God brought forth Christian-centered individuals to share testimonies of afflictions that, by God's grace, I have not experienced. Those testimonies brought wisdom proceeding how to understand those situations, allowing me to expand my ministry beyond my experiences. Now, I stand in faith knowing that all that God brings me to, He will bring me through. It was then that God began to use me and I began to see victory in my season.

The difficult truth about victory is that it only comes after a battle. In all battles God will protect, give grace, and allow access to His people. God will allow trauma, so His people can learn how to access Him at all times.

> "for he is our God. We are the people he watches over, the flock under his care. If only you would listen to his voice today!"
>
> -Psalm 95:7

It is often presented as if God throws us in arena and watches us proceed with traumatic events. We ass Christians often have the Job complex. We tell ourselves that we were as faithful and honorable as Job, and that we are unjustly assigned trials and tribulations. The reality is that we are often disobedient to God's word, getting ourselves in situations. God, being as loving as He is, uses the blood of Jesus to protect us. Now, I am going to explain this in multiple ways because this concept is difficult for many to accept.

For my audience that has a love for science, affliction is a germ. While that germ is our battle that we got from our actions of being in a germ-infested area, we cough and feel as if the symptoms we are fighting alone. In reality, the blood of Jesus is our white blood cells and actually battling the germ. The cold symptoms are just evidence of God moving in our lives. For those that have an interest in sports, it is similar to a quarterback taking too long to throw the ball. The quarterback got himself in the position to be sacked by stalling with the ball, yet feels alone on that field. In reality, the blood of Jesus is the linemen that is keeping the trials from taking over. The pressure we feel is just evidence of God moving in our lives. Another example for those that understand things in terms of money. We often think financial attacks are sent straight from the enemy. We pray and feel God is watching us struggle. In reality, our financial struggles are the result of us not using money for God's glory leading to debt, not knowing that the blood of Jesus is our inheritance. Our "inheritance" is accessible through access to the power of God.

"The Spirit of the Lord is upon me, for he has anointed me to bring Good News to the poor. He has sent me to proclaim that captives will be released, that the blind will see, that the oppressed will be set free,

19   and that the time of the Lord's favor has come."

-Luke 4:18-19

With the anointing, God will give us status. This status allows us to have favor with the Lord and see victory. This is when it is important to fellowship with others. One may pray and not see victory in a battle that you are facing, however, praying with an elder in a church that is anointed in victory over the affliction you are facing. That elder could be anointed not only because they have previously fought the battle, but they stood in faith, as tears rolled down their cheeks and gained favor by God. That elder may have a status that you just have not earned yet. Yet, when one is anointed God will allow you access to His power individually or by proxy. When you do not have anyone to pray with during time of need, praying:

"God, I come before you in this time of need asking for forgiveness, but also asking for access to your power. Lord, may the power of the blood that resides in me come out of me and heal me."

Praying this will either allow access to God's power or give access to God's grace.

> "In that day the Lord will end the bondage of his people. He will break the yoke of slavery and lift it from their shoulders."
>
> -Isaiah 10:27

As stated before, we often get ourselves in situations caused by direct disobedience to God. Situations that could destroy us, God uses His grace to protect us from because He has a use for us. There was an instance when I was with a man that I knew better than to spend time with. We had built a relationship based in sin. The entire time that I was in that man's presence, I had anxiety. This man caused chaos in my home, as well as his.

Upon ending the toxic relationship, the man began to call and text me non-stop. He made threats against me and my family. The threats began to affect my work life. That situation could have ended me financially and emotionally, yet God gave me grace. None of the threats were acted upon and I received a pay increase. I received that victory in the name of Jesus and I praised until the next victory.

Once God is able to use you, victory becomes a lifestyle. The lifestyle of victory consists of:

- Consistent success
- Maintaining a mind of winning
- Adaptability to the will of God
- Purpose driven life

"And she said, 'Father, if you have made a vow to the Lord, you must do to me what you have vowed, for the Lord has given you a great victory over your enemies'..."
-Judges 11:36

We know that in the midst of our tears, we make vows to God. The vows are pleas for grace and mercy in exchange for devotion to God. To remain in a season of victory we must honor those vows with submission. Ask God what he wants you to do. Ask God what your next steps should be. This shows God that you honor Him with not only flexibility, but also in faith. Next, ask God to show if you aree in the way of your next miracle. Actions that do not align with Christian values can delay miracles. Request that God remove those who are not believers and cannot assist in your walk with God. With all miracles, change is bound to happen. This change will bring about a challenge. Request that God makes you seek more than the mediocre. God is not one that moves in typical lifestyles. He receives the glory from the testimonies of greatness! If fear is preventing you from seeking the greatness of God, then you are missing the miracles. A victory prayer I use is:

> "God, I come before you knowing that I am shielded by the blood of Jesus, seeking guidance. My vow to victory is only valid if I

seek a true walk of faith. Lord, what shall be my next steps in this journey? God, empty my spirit of worldly comforts. Fill me with your desires, so that I am not delaying my miracles. Please remove anything or anyone that influences my belief in you. God, use me in a way that my testimony will be evidence of your greatness. Lord, let mediocrity be scarce in my life, and let victory become second nature. Mold me as you see fit."

The lifestyle of victory will move you into your season of milk and honey. The year of 2025 began the season of milk and honey for not only myself, but many other C.H.A.N.G.E.D Church members.

"7 For the Lord your God is bringing you into a good land of flowing streams and pools of water, with fountains and springs that gush out in the valleys and hills. 8 It is a land of wheat and barley; of grapevines, fig trees, and pomegranates; of olive oil and honey. 9 It is a land where food is plentiful and nothing is lacking. It is a land where iron is as common as stone, and copper is abundant in the hills. ¹⁰ When you have eaten your fill, be sure to praise the Lord your God for the good land he has given you."

-Deuteronomy 8:7-10

Milk is symbolic for the results of your effort. Honey is strictly blessings that coincidently stumble upon. In the first three months of my season of milk and honey, I witnessed the evidence of this season of victory. My "milk" was the pay increase that came from taking professional development courses. I also watched the opportunities for my starter business expand. The very completion and publishing of this book is part of my "milk". My honey was evident in the connections that I made during this season. To walk in obedience, I was required to complete and publish this book. I never considered writing as a career choice, so I lacked the knowledge about publishing a book. My "honey" was the support for my church family. Many of the women that I fellowshipped with are published authors. They guided me through the steps of publishing a book while avoiding financial scams. I also found "honey" in connections with my educational career. While starting my own educational facility, I connected with a founder in the Perris Unified School District. This woman had knowledge of government funding and promotion within the district. Her connections, combined with leaders of a S.T.E.M camp, that my son attended, gave me the opportunities that I prayed for. The "honey" brought upon opportunities to expand financially, yet more importantly, I was also able to expand my ministry. The more opportunities that I had to connect with people, the more I was able to testify all that God has done for me.

"I will bring that group through the fire and make them pure. I will refine them like silver and purify them like gold. They will call on my name, and I will answer them. I will say, 'These are my people,' and they will say, 'The Lord is our God.'"

-Zechariah 13:9

Those that God can use are gold to Him. No matter the condition of gold it is always of value. Even when we come before God broken and sinful, we are still gold. Though God may use the fire of pressure to refine us and make us more flexible to His demands, we always will hold value. Our testimony, gives God the glory and there is nothing greater that we can offer Him.

www.ingramcontent.com/pod-product-compliance
Lightning Source LLC
Chambersburg PA
CBHW081539120626
46550CB00009B/2793